Books used to help write this book:

—Webster's New World Dictionary
—NIV Holy Bible
—The Gideon's Holy Bible

TAKE OFF
THE MASK

You can fool people some of the time,
but you can't fool God at anytime

LYNETTE EDWARDS

Order this book online at www.trafford.com
or email orders@trafford.com

Most Trafford titles are also available at major online book retailers.

Printed in the United States of America.

ISBN: 978-1-4669-1974-7 (sc)
ISBN: 978-1-4669-1976-1 (hc)
ISBN: 978-1-4669-1975-4 (e)

Library of Congress Control Number: 2012904562

Trafford rev. 03/12/2012

www.trafford.com

North America & international
toll-free: 1 888 232 4444 (USA & Canada)
phone: 250 383 6864 ♦ fax: 812 355 4082

CONTENTS

ACKNOWLEDGEMENTS

To God be the glory! He is truly a wonder in my soul, the love of my life, and guide to my pathway to heaven. God has been better to me than I have been to myself. He has opened doors that no man can close, and closed doors that no man can open. There is something about the name of Jesus that sets my soul on fire. He is the reason I live.

To my dad, Wyldon Edwards, who has sacrificed his life to raise me, you are my hero. To my mom, Birdie Edwards, I love you and pray for you daily.

To my sisters Precious Boudreaux and Kayla Minix, there is a bond between us that I pray will never be broken. All of our tests are now miraculous testimonies.

To my nieces Kennedi and Kendall Boudreaux, God has something truly special in store for you and my prayer is that you keep God first and allow him to mature you both into respectful, loving, spirit filled young ladies.

To Darrell Boudreaux and Christopher Minix, may God allow you to be the head of your homes and love your families as Christ loves the church.

To the Riggs family; Minister Murphy, Latonia, Kirsten Isaiah, and Ayden you are truly a blessing from God and my prayer is that God would allow you to set an example for others as you live the lives you were created to live.

To my cousins (Brandy, Amirah, John, Summer, Chloe, Phillip Jr., Brandon, Candice, Madison, Randy, Keedra, and Rhonda(Peaches), friends, Gussman Photography, and my Progressive Baptist church family thank you for everything that you have done for me, whether an encouraging word, or smile on your face; I humbly thank you.

To the one person that has fed me with spiritual bread during the times in my life that I needed it the most, Pastor Lloyd Joiner, Jr.; thank you. You are truly a gift from God and my prayer is that he will bless you beyond your expectations. May God bless you and your family and be a hedge of protection around you always.

TAKE OFF THE MASK

Bold, gifted, tall, loud, humble, courageous, nervous, shy, motivated, multi talented, quiet, determined, optimistic, patient, ambitious; whoever you are it's time to be the best that you can be. No need for you to feel as though you must put on a show or act as though you have to be who the world expects you to become. It is time to hold your head up high and walk with Christ and become the person that he predestined you to be.

It is time for you to take off the mask. Be free. Be unique. Be you.

I am daring you right now to start unveiling the true you one layer at a time. Because when you unveil who you are, it is then that you can become the person you were created to be. God is able to turn your darkness into sunshine, jealousy into joy, and pain into peace. He is more than able which means he is available beyond limited expectations to do exceedingly more than you can ask or imagine. You have covered up for too long and today is the day for you to be free.

You can fool people some of the time but I promise you that God can't be fooled any of the time. What are you waiting for? It's time to firmly yet gracefully take off the mask!

CHAPTER 1

He that has started a good work in you will complete what he has begun

I like most people, love to try many different things. The start of a new project sounds exciting and fun yet once reality sets in that it isn't as easy as I imagined it to be; I quit. I then try to justify why the last project didn't work and convince myself that there is something else better for me to do. The only problem is that just like the first time I eventually end up getting tired and I quit. It is not that I couldn't do it but I have now made up excuses why I don't want to do it. Let me tell you something. A justification is just an excuse to why you don't finish what you start. I know you get tired, I get tired too. I know you are scarred, well I get scarred too. I know it is hard work; newsflash nothing in this life with the exception of salvation is free. We must learn to finish what we start. When we accept Jesus into our hearts it isn't a one day commitment. In fact it is a twenty four hour, seven day a week, three hundred sixty five day a year commitment. How do we stay committed? I am glad you want to know. The answer is simple but takes much work. Are you ready for the answer? Can you handle the truth? Sit down relax and let me give it to you straight. You must learn that it is not about you. Matthew 16:24 states: "Then Jesus said to his disciples, 'If anyone would come after me, he must deny himself, and take up his cross, and follow me." That verse simply means that you have to give yourself away so that you may be fully used for the glory of the Lord. Aren't you tired running in circles? Don't you get tired starting and giving up? Jesus wants you to deny yourself and willingly come to him so that he can complete the work that he has already purposely started in you.

When a teenager finishes high school and goes off to college they may deicide to go for a nurse, study three years then change their major to an engineer then get tired of the studying and classes and quit school. It is not that the individual doesn't want to get educated or want better for their lives but one of the most common reasons they quit is because they are tired. Their body is aching from waking up early and staying up until midnight to study. They feel as though they are giving up everything for school yet missing time that can be spent with family and friends. So they make a decision to quit. What they didn't realize is that they, just like you and I, alone do not have everything we need to make it. We need help. We don't need the help of a parent or sibling. We don't need the help of a counselor or teacher. We need the help of the almighty, all powerful, everlasting, sweet spirited God. We need him to wrap his arms around us when we are lonely, give us strength when we are tired, cover us when we are afraid. It is then with the presence of God that we are able to keep pressing forward. We are able to finish all the work that we started because greater is he that is in us then he that is in this world.

I have to personally remind myself that I didn't have anything to do with the work that was started in me. In fact if it was up to me I wouldn't be living the life that God has predestined me to live.

I would probably be working two or three jobs looking out of the window hoping and wishing and praying that something better would come along not realizing that if I want better I have to go out and get it. In other words if I can't find a job doing what I love then I can open up my own business. I can be my own boss. I can work my own hours. I can sign my own checks. Why? Because I am royalty. We must learn our worth. I may not be a size two model or have the beauty of Miss America but I love me and if you don't like what you see when you look my way you have the option of turning your head in the opposite direction.

When you take off the mask you will find something so beautiful and loving. When you take off the mask you will find yourself. A person who is made in the image and likeness of a God who could have created you to be anything and look any way yet he decided to make you just as you are. Excuse me for a minute but to me that is shouting news. God could have done anything with me yet he took me to the secret place and he chose to make me just like I am. Now why on earth would you want to tamper with such a lovely creation? I don't know the last time you looked in the mirror but when I look I see something pass the freckles on my face. I am more then what the eyes meet. I look at myself and see someone who is unique and there is no one in the world exactly like me.

I can't afford not to be me because there is no one who can do what I was called to do. I used to always sit and wonder how one person could do so much work in their life and I would get mad at the fact that God would allow one person to accomplish so much while another accomplished much of nothing. But then I realized that even if the person who has already done so much would stop, then the work that they were called to do would stop know when the. Why? Because no one can do the assignment that God has placed in your heart for you to do. He has perfectly equipped you with all that you need to run your race in life. God has given you faith that should be able to move mountains, trust that allows you to lean and depend on him, wisdom that assist with the making of sound decisions, peace that surpasses all human understanding and the holy spirit that stands up in you. In fact he promised that he would never put more on us then we can bear. However, as great as that may sound don't get too excited because God does not need you. Just in case you didn't hear me clearly let me repeat what I just said; GOD DOES NOT NEED YOU. God is able to use anything and anybody. In fact he once opened the mouth of a donkey and even made a stone cry out. You have to understand that even though God can use anything and anyone God did choose you to go out and do works for his kingdom. In fact John 15:16 states: "You have not chosen me, but I chose you and ordained you, that you may go and bring fruit, and that your fruit should remain: that whatsoever you shall ask of the Father in my name, he may give it to you."

But you must remember that it will be hard to do good works when your face is covered with a mask.

Yet as powerful and great as our God is he will never force you to follow him. Instead he will wait patiently for you to make a conscious choice and decide which path you want to follow. There is a path that will take you through heart break and failure, you will have limited success, and you will never truly understand who you are or why you were put on this earth for such a time as this. But then there is a path that will lead you to real love. A path that will show you how one made the ultimate sacrifice and because of that selfless act of love you can now have peace that surpasses all human understanding and joy that people of the world will never truly understand and then after this life is over if you chose the right path you will live a life of eternity. The choice is completely yours. You can't wait until tomorrow for tomorrow is not promised. You have to make a choice today. In fact you must choose this day whom you will serve. It is when you make a decision that you are able to finish all that you start because you will have the only one that is able to keep you from falling living inside of you.

I did not start this work in my life but thankfully by the grace and mercy of God I will willingly deny myself and allow him to finish the work that he started. I will let him show me the plans that he has for me then like a helpless sheep looking for a Sheppard I will continue to follow him until my work on this earth is done and it is time for me to go to my heavenly home.

CHAPTER 2

Pulling off the mask one layer at a time

There is a mask that many people wear at church, you walk in the sanctuary with your two piece suit, head in the air wearing the latest fashion. You walk up to every member that you know gently kiss them on the cheek Speaking in your proper voice you talk about what a wonderful week you have had and how perfect your life is, you talk about the goodness of the Lord and quote your favorite scripture. You put on a show as though you are living the life of an above average theology professor who spends every waking moment with the Lord, when the truth is that you don't open your bible outside of church service, you have gossiped about every member at the church and you wouldn't know Gods' voice if he screamed in your right ear and told you who he was. For some reason, that is unknown to me you put on a mask in front of others. Not that you have to but because you made a decision to. Now whether you wear a mask because you don't like the person underneath the mask or you wear it because you are too fearful to be whom you truly are it's time to slowly yet firmly take off the mask.

In Hebrews 12:1 it says "Wherefore seeing we also are compassed about with so great a cloud of witnesses, let us lay aside every weight, and the sin which do so easily beset us, and let us run with patience the race that is set before us."

We as Christians must lay down all weight. It is nearly impossible to run a race all the way to the finish line carrying excess weight. All you are doing is making it harder on yourself. Are you hiding behind sin? If so repent to your heavenly father. He said he would cast our sins as far as the east is from the west. The east and west never meet up which means that he will never bring up your sin or hinder it from allowing you to move forward. Are you hiding because of low self confident? You have to believe in yourself. In fact I am my biggest cheerleader. You must learn to encourage yourself. Through the tears, through the pain, through the trials and tribulations you must pat your own self on the back and believe that every test will turn into a miraculous testimony. Are you hiding because of fear? God is able to turn your fear into faith. He is able to work with faith as small as a mustard seed. A mustard seed is the smallest seed planted yet it grows into the biggest in the field. God can give you more faith than you can even envision. Are you hiding because of doubt? God can turn your doubt into deliverance. He is more than able to do it. In fact he is patiently waiting on you to call his name. Are you hiding because of pride? If so he can make you humble in a way that you will reverence him and bow down before his presence just for who he is. Are you hiding because of the past? Each day is new. There is no need to live in yesterday for God has already given you a new day and he is able to renew you, restore you, and revive you. What exactly are you hiding from? Whatever it is big or small there is nothing, and I mean nothing that our God can't do if you simply believe.

It truly saddens me when I see people who want to humbly come to Christ but just do not know how to, so for a minute let me explain to you how easy it is. When you simply confess with your mouth and believe in your heart that Jesus died for you then you too will be saved and inherit the kingdom. Once you are saved there is no turning back. You can't straddle the fence. You must move forward. You have to understand that every saint has a past and all sinners have a future. Don't assume for one minute that the person next to you is perfect for the bible clearly tells us in Romans 3:23, "For All have sinned and come short of the gory of God." The problem is that we as Christians don't always talk about our sins instead we walk around as though we are holier then thou and don't take the time to remember that we too are nothing but unworthy rags not fit to live and hardly close to being ready to die.

It's time that we start telling it like it is. For those of you who don't quite understand let me be the first to show you what I mean when I say "tell it like it is". My name is Lynette Edwards; I wasn't born with a silver spoon in my mouth. I have gone to bed hungry from not having the money to buy food. I have literally spent the night in an apartment with no electricity because I couldn't pay my light bill. I have had to catch a cab to go to work, walk home because of not having a ride, borrow money from family, thought about compromising my integrity just to pay my rent. I have had to cry more times than I can remember and doubted if I wanted to live to see my tomorrows more times than I can count. I have been sick and had to have a surgery for bad eating habits, I have had to go through excruciating dental work because of pain in my gums, been misused on the job, overworked and underpaid, back stabbed, talked about by family and so called friends, cheated on, talked down to, I have even contemplated suicide. But through all of the hurt, tears, downs, failure, heartache, and pain by the grace and love of God I am still here.

I refuse to wear a mask. I may not be perfect, God knows I have made my share of mistakes but one thing I am proud to say is that through it all I never lost my praise!

If you are reading this book that means that you have breath in your body. And since you are still alive it's not by accident or coincidence. You are still alive because God has work for you to do. Too often we let situations and people hinder the work that is needed to be done. I know you have your own agenda but for a moment I need you to get off of your high horse and be about your fathers' business.

Taking layers off is never easy in fact it will be one of the hardest things you may ever have to do. But can you just sit for a moment and think about how great you will be and how wonderful you will feel when you allow yourself to be free. It will be as though you lost one hundred pounds without having to visit a gym. I get excited just thinking about it. I don't know how you feel about it but I feel like completely and totally letting go and letting God. I mean no offense but I refuse to wait until I die to get some heaven. In fact I want heaven on earth. Can you imagine waking up on this side and not having to worry about anything? You can wake up rejoicing because you have enough faith to believe that your father in heaven has already worked everything out. My, what a time you will have when you can forget about the troubles of this world and focus on the joys of heaven.

Someone told me that they are scarred to die. I wanted to sit and cry because that person is so wrapped up in her fears of dying that she is missing out on living. This life can take you many different places and you can feel millions of different emotions but you have to be willing to live. Go out and see the wonders of the land and how amazing this earth truly is. There is so much out there that it truly does take a lifetime to see. I hope you are bold enough to peel off every layer in time so that you don't miss anything.

But be careful not to peel to fast or you may find your self worse off than you were before. Why? Because if you have not totally let go and released everything to God then you will find your self missing and wanting what once hindered you. The bible tells us in Matthew 26:41 states "Watch and pray so that you don't fall into temptation for the spirit is willing but the flesh is weak." That verse simply means that we have to always be on guard and we must be willing to follow the spirit if not the flesh will lead you.

Remember that you can not be spirit led until you are spirit fed.

CHAPTER 3

What's done in the dark will come to the light

What tangled webs we weave. We party all night Saturday then rush to the church house on Sunday. We get drunk on Friday than quote scriptures on Monday. Husbands swap wives and wives swap husbands all night long, yet in the early morning light we have the nerve to judge someone else for the life they live. I have said it once and I will say it again, you may be able to fool people some of the time but I promise you, you can not ffool God any of the time.

It surprises me how people will carry on at parties but when a preacher/teacher of the gospel walks in everyone hides their alcohol and changes their conversation. I am glad that there is a respect for that preacher/teacher but do you not know that God was in the room before that preacher showed up? God is omnipresent which means he is present at all places at the same time. He sees all, knows all, and hears all. There is no hiding from him. No making up lies to cover your tracks. God has been watching you since the day you were born in fact Jeremiah 1:5 says, "Before I formed you in the womb I knew you, before you were born I set you apart; I appointed you as a prophet to the nations." Who do you think you are that you can hide from the all mighty, all powerful omnipotent God? I am here to tell you that it just can't be done. He is miraculously everywhere.

Now I know you are smart and articulate, I understand that you finished high school at the top of the class, remained on the dean's list in college, and have a PhD but I am here to tell you that you still can't outsmart God. He saw you when you sinned on yesterday and will be watching when you purposely commit sin on tomorrow. But what is so great about our God is that his anger is but for a moment and his loving favor last for an entire lifetime.

His anger is for a moment; that is truly amazing. That simple means that God knows how to let go and look past that moment. The problem with a lot of us is that we hold on to situations that we truly need to let go. I spent years with built up anger and rage because of events from my past. It is hard to let go of hurt, pain, anger, and betrayal. But you have to remember that you can't run your race with baggage. You have to lay it down and move forward. Stop letting trials and life's tribulations stop the smile on your face. You are holding on to anger while the person who hurt you is enjoying their life. Let go! Move on! If a God who is the creator of the universe can forgive you of all of your transgressions then why on the face of God's green earth are you still holding on to your past. I made up my mind a few years ago that I was going to move forward. In fact I was at a conference when the speaker began talking about forgiveness and life after the pain.

As she spoke I sat in my seat and cried like a baby. I was well in my twenties and I was still holding on to childhood memories. I raised my hand and asked this question, "How do you ask a person for forgiveness when the person doesn't know that they have hurt you?" Before the speaker could answer me I broke down crying and soon after I had the speaker and attendees at the conference in tears also. I had to learn that forgiveness isn't for the other person; it is for you. I forgave the person who hurt me in my heart and once I did I felt as though one thousand pounds were lifted from my shoulders. I felt like I could fly as high as an eagle and run faster than any animal in the wild. I was finally freed from my past. Philippians 3:13-14 states, "Brothers, I do not consider myself yet to have taken hold of it. But one thing I do: Forgetting what is behind and straining toward what is ahead. I press on toward the goal to win the prize for which God has called me heavenward in Christ Jesus". We all must press forward. When I imagine pressing forward I envision my heavenly father waiting with open arms. I can see white doves flying and angels rejoicing. When I envision pressing forward I see the cross that Jesus once hung on and how his sweet spirit is omnipresent. Pressing forward brings me peace and happiness.

But one thing that doesn't bring true happiness is when we walk in darkness. Have you ever walked into a room without the lights being on? You hit your foot on tables and chairs; hold out your hands to feel your way through the room. It is terrifying to know that you can't see ahead yet so many of us purposely walk in darkness. You can see with your eyes but you are spiritually blinded. Unfortunately you have become stuck in your darkness and are too fearful to get out. What is your fear? What are you letting stop your joy and block your blessings? It is one thing to be stuck in the dark because you haven't paid a light bill or because there is bad weather and all the lights are out but for you to choose to walk freely in the dark because you don't think you have what it takes to walk in the light, that my friend is sad. You have the power to choose. I hope you choose wisely because Jesus is real. His love is real. His peace is real. In fact everything good comes from him. There isn't enough minutes in the day, sand on the beach, or animals in the zoo for me to begin to describe how real my God is. Don't take my word go out and try him for yourself.

There is truly something special about the name Jesus. He is a wonder in my soul. He is the light of my life, joy of my world, lover of my heart. It's good to know him. In fact I can't even begin to imagine my life without him. I smile at the mention of him and rejoice in his presence. My God what a privilege it is to be a child of the most high.

CHAPTER 4

Stop playing Church

"At least I got it over with" was the words I heard walking out of a respectable church in the state where I reside. I turned and to my surprise was a middle aged woman standing there with a grin on her face because Sunday morning worship service was over. I was stunned as I stood at a stand still while the words that she said were still playing over in my head. What in the world does she mean she got it over with? Did she not take heed to the teaching that was done? Did she not feel the Holy Spirit move in that sanctuary? Wow, totally speechless.

Sadly that is the attitude of a lot of Christians today. We go to church just to get it over with. We don't go because we want to be fed or we want a fresh anointing to fall fresh on us, but instead we attend church so that we can simply "get it over with". Then we go home and wonder why we go through so much hell on earth. It may be because we didn't ask God to regulate our mind and allow us to take heed to the worship service. There is a time in our lives that we simply have to grow up. We can't do the same things we once did or live life as though we still have the mindset of a child. It's one thing for a young child to not like church because they don't understand the word of God or because he or she feels as though their parents are forcing them to go, but for a mature minded woman or man of God to walk around and play church, excuse me but in my opinion that is unacceptable.

You have to find your set place and the only way you can do that is by allowing God to show you where it is. You may indeed be attending the wrong place of worship which may easily cause you to be distracted and uninterested in the service. Whatever your religion may be, you have to find the right church for you so that you may begin a relationship with God and then wait for him to guide you and nurture you. So many of us join churches out of tradition and attend out of habit. Then we stay because we don't want people to talk about us. Well I don't know if you are naïve or not but people are already talking about you. In fact people will talk about you until the day you die and then beyond the grave. My point is people will be people. And if that is a reason you are staying in the place you are in you need to move on. Jeremiah 29:11 states: "For I know the plans I have for you" declares the Lord, "plans to prosper you and not harm you, plans to give you hope and a future." I never in a million years imagined being an author, speaker, playwright, counselor, or owning a religious non profit organization but thank God that his plans were far better than the plans that I had for my self. But the only reason I know that his plans were better is because I gave myself away to him and humbly allowed him to use me for his glory.

I refrained from looking at what I planned and what I wanted and sought him in all of my ways and made up my mind to be receptive to what he told me. In fact my prayer is that God will use me until he can't use me anymore. For I know that when I am being used by God everything works out for my good. It doesn't matter what the day holds as long as my heavenly father in heaven holds me in the palm of his hands all is well.

I would be remiss if I told you to follow God's plan but didn't tell you how to let go of your plans to follow his. It is very simple words but can be very hard to do. Are you ready? Have you made up your mind that you are tired making your own plans and trying to do things in your own mite and power? It is very simple to follow him; you must get your mind set on Jesus. Philippians 2:5 states: "Your attitude should be the same as that of Christ Jesus." If your mind is on Jesus you will have the desire to please him and follow his plans. Your mind determines your thoughts, your thoughts determine your talk, your talk determines your walk and your walk determines your action, to make it plain and simple; get your mind right.

Your mind is so powerful that is why you must pray diligently that God regulates your mind daily. You need to have the mindset of Jesus to be able to understand what he has placed you on this earth to do. Don't get it twisted for you will never know all of the thoughts and wonders of our God. But by keeping your mind regulated you are able to get to know him in a way that allows you to follow his plans for your wonderful life.

I struggled with this for a long time. It is far more easily said than done. There are so many distractions that it is easy to stray away. But like anything you have to make up your mind to stay focused at all times. Because even though you sleep the enemy doesn't and if he could have your mind he knows that the rest of you is sure to follow. There were times when I thought that I was going crazy as I battled with staying focused but by mentioning the name Jesus all would be well. Jesus doesn't have facebook, nor does he have a twitter account, he doesn't even carry a cell phone, but at the mention of his name he comes to your rescue quicker than right now and sooner than later. He wraps his loving arms around you and holds you in a way that only a father can. He then in his own way reassures you that everything will be alright. My, what a mighty God we serve. I wish I could yell it on top of every building of the world. He is truly a wonder in my soul. Heaven and earth shall pass away but the word of God will last forever and ever.

Stop playing church. Get your relationship right with the Lord today for no man knows the day or hour of his final death nor do we know when Jesus is going to return. All you have is this present moment. It's as easy as confessing with your mouth and believing in your heart that God is real and that Jesus has died for your sins. Repeat these simple words, Lord I confess with my mouth and believe in my heart that Jesus died for me and that all my sins are forgiven, and you too are now saved and have no earthly excuse to play church.

CHAPTER 5

Hollow Christians

Every Easter there are millions of eatable Easter bunnies made. Some of chocolate, others of marsh mellows. My personal favorite is a dark chocolate Easter bunny filled with pecans and caramels. Those are the ones that you just sit back, relax and enjoy because it is filled with way more on the inside than what is on the outside. But then every now and again when you go to the store, you walk past your favorite chocolate bunny to one that is simply beautiful on the outside. You decide to purchase it and take it home only to find that when you bite inside of it, the bunny is empty. There is nothing but hollow chocolate inside. Talk about disappointing. Well unfortunately the Easter bunny isn't the only thing that is hollow. Take a good look in the mirror my friend and tell me what you have inside.

I know you dress well, you ladies have the purse to match the shoes, fellows have the neck tie with matching handkerchief but I want to know what exactly is on the inside. Are you filled with darkness and a void, maybe jealousy and pain? Whatever it is that has you hollow you need to lay it down and let it loose because you can fool people some of the time but I promise you that God can't be fooled at anytime.

How can I fill my hollow with holiness? I am so glad you asked. James 1:22 states, "Be doers of the word, and not hearers only, deceiving your own selves." It is one thing for you to be able to quote scriptures but what good is it if you don't live by them. Filling yourself with holiness requires some alone time with God. It's more than just a Sunday morning worship or Wednesday night praise, it is truly a lifestyle. You have to learn to sacrifice yourself to the Lord. Go to your secret closet and pour out your heart and soul. Let you father in heaven know how you truly feel and how much you long to be closer to him. You have to take the first step and believe that God will meet you right where you are. No matter what condition (spiritually or mentally) God is more than able to fill your cup beyond your imaginations. But it takes daily commitment and you have to be able to stand because the enemy will come at you during your weakest moments like a bat out of hell doing all that he can to stop you. In order to stand through it all you must know your weak areas and then guard those areas with all of your might because evil is always present. He comes to steal, kill, and destroy. Many times we get big headed thinking we have everything figured out and that we can do it without getting attacked but you have to understand that the devil is real and that he wants nothing more than to devour you.

But take heed my Christian friend because just as the enemy is real so is God. You have to know and believe that the Holy Spirit lives inside of you and if you believe that God is stronger than the enemy then there is nothing that the enemy can do to you. No weapon formed shall prosper. Now that doesn't mean that weapons won't be formed, because trust me they will. But no weapon shall prosper because God promised in Romans 8:28,

"And we know that all things work together for good to them that love God, to them who are the called according to his purpose."

I hope you didn't miss your opportunity to shout because I don't know about you but knowing that God works out everything for my good makes me shout praises onto him. My God how awesome is thee. Knowing that I have God on my side makes my days brighter, I can walk with my head held high because I know that he is more than able to keep me from falling. The word able A B L E to me stands for Available Beyond Limited Expectations. There is nothing to hard for my God. The sea can't drown him, man can't stop him, bullets can't kill him, Satan can't attack him, demons can't posses him, and the grave can't hold him.

He is God and God all be himself. I know you think he needs you. Newsflash, he doesn't. He doesn't need you to play church or put your two cents in the collection basket. Instead he wants you. He wants you to make a conscious decision and willingly go to him. He has so much love to give that man can't even begin to envision. He wants all of you and he truly deserves it. There is no one that I know on the face of this earth that will live a sacrificial life than get brutally assaulted, beaten, and then humbly die; No one but Jesus.

The first time I saw the movie the Passion of the Christ I wept uncontrollably. I had so much emotions going through my body. To have to watch someone you love go through so much for someone as unworthy as yourself was too much for me and to know that he did it willingly; my God. I went from being angry and hurt to feeling sick to my stomach by the way Jesus was treated.

Yet in all I can now rejoice because he did it for me. He did it for you. He did it so that we can live a life full of abundance and have eternal rest. He did it so that we can have peace that surpasses all human understanding, joy that the world didn't give and the world can never take away. He did it because of love.

CHAPTER 6

Closet Christian

There are a group of teenagers that love the Lord. In church they sing praises from the top of their lungs and sit quietly as they await the preachers' sermon. But on Monday morning at school they hang around the popular kids laughing and joking at those teenagers that are not as popular as they are. They participate in fornication and live a life in a way that they can be accepted by their peers. They forget who they are and get lost among the crowd. Then they hurry to the bathroom and in secret pray that God forgives them for how they don't stand up for what is right. They know in their heart what is right but don't quite understand how to come out of the closet.

Unfortunately these teenagers aren't the only ones that are closet Christians. There are adults, some your co workers and friends who like these teenagers don't know how to come out and take a stand for Christ. There is one thing that stops us all from being free and taking a stand. That one thing is fear. Fear as defined in Webster's New World dictionary is an unpleasant often strong emotion caused by the expectation or awareness of danger, also: an instance of or a state marked by this emotion.

Working a job with different people who share different religious backgrounds can make you feel as though you have to hide your religion, and that can be quite awkward. I remember dealing with a situation at work and instead of being able to verbally voice what I was feeling I had to go to the bathroom, get on my knees, and pray. The second I heard someone coming I would hurry up and pretend to be washing my hands so that they didn't find out what I was doing. I was too fearful of what might have happened if I was caught on my knees praying to God. Never once was I bold enough to sing praises to God or talk about how good God is and how he has stepped in every time I needed him. Instead I would pray in my head and then sit at the table and gossip with everyone and talk about everything that they wanted to hear just to fit in because I was too afraid to be me and talk about the goodness of God. I was locked in fear.

Fear is what keeps up from moving forward, Fear keeps us in our comfort zone and allows us to do just enough to make it without having to take a stand. Thankfully we as Christians have the power to replace our fear with faith. Faith is simply the substance of things hoped for and the evidence of things not seen. Faith is saying I can walk on water but can't see how deep the sea is. Faith is saying I can move a mountain without physically moving it. Faith is saying that you believe. You have to believe in yourself and believe that God's power is stronger than any other power in this universe. You have to take a stand and not be ashamed of the gospel of the Lord. He wasn't ashamed when he fasted forty days and forty nights. He wasn't ashamed when he humbly hung on a cross and died for you. You should be able to stand proud, talk about the goodness of the Lord, and come out of the closet.

I used to be a closet Christian. As much as I loved the Lord and all that he stands for I was afraid of what my family and friends would think of me if I started living right and talking about church. I would use excessive profanity, fornicate, and go to night clubs. But I got tired; tired of pretending just to fit in. I would go to clubs and stand in the corner praying that my friends would suggest that we go home. I would purposely fornicate just not to have the man that I was involved with leave me. And it wasn't that I didn't like having sex, trust me I did. But I couldn't even enjoy it because of the guilt I felt from knowing that God would not be pleased with the way his child was behaving. One day I woke up and decided that I was going to live for God. I wasn't going to worry myself with what people said or if the man I loved left me. I was determined to be that Christian that when God looked at me he smiled. I slowly refrained from the gossiping and partying. And as hard as it was I gave up sex. Part of me still can't believe I was able to give it up but I had purposely made up my mind to live a life accordingly. I lost friends, boyfriends, and even some that I knew questioned my lifestyle but I knew that I had to be free from the purposeful sin that I was committing. I am not saying that I am perfect for Romans 3:23 states: "For all have sinned and fall short of the glory of God", but I am trying to make positive decisions for my today so that I can experience a better tomorrow.

You can make better decisions when you take a stand for what you believe. Stop living in fear. You need to pray so that you can be freed and start living a productive life without worrying what people will think because even though there are millions of daily choices to make, there are only two choices to where you will spend eternity; heaven or hell

CHAPTER 7

Riding in the second chariot

Have you ever heard the saying too many chiefs and not enough Indians? It is a very popular saying used to describe how everyone wants to be the boss. No one wants to sit in the back seat instead we all want to drive. The problem is there is only room for one driver. No car has two steering wheels if they did there would be nothing but turmoil and confusion because we all have different directions that we want to travel. So instead there is a driver seat and a passenger seat and for all others who want to join the ride you can comfortable sit in the back seat. There is nothing wrong with being the passenger. You can sit and relax and assist the driver when needed. You don't have to worry about being liable if there is an accident and you aren't held accountable if you don't make it to your destination in a timely manner. You can sit back, relax, and enjoy the ride.

So why does everyone want to drive? One word, control! The driver controls where you go, what turns you make, and what time you make it to your destination. The downside to being the driver is nothing compared to the feeling you get when you are actually in control.

There is absolutely nothing wrong with riding in the second chariot. In fact if you move to the driver seat before you are called there you may cause confusion and miss the blessings that were destined for you. I know it looks exciting to let the wind blow through your hair as people see you behind the wheel but you have to know that if you are in your set place you will get an overflow of blessing. In fact the blessings from the driver will flow on you in addition to the blessings that are already yours. So let's figure it out, you can sit in the passenger seat, listen to the sweet sounds of the radio, and relax or you can be someone who drives through the traffic, rushing to make it to the destination on time worrying about not getting hit by an oncoming vehicle. Pardon me but why does everyone want to be the boss again?

Since working in ministry I have seen and heard some things that I can't even begin to describe. From so called Christians hoping someone gets bumped out of leadership to Christians back talking and gossiping about the leader they have because they personally believe that they can do a better job at leading. No offense but if God wanted you to lead a ministry or job he would have put you in the place to be a leader.

We must stop putting ourselves in places that we feel is best for us. You don't have to have authority to be blessed as those in authority are blessed. All you have to do is let the work that you do speak for itself. If you are a ditch digger than go out and be the best ditch digger you can possibly be. Don't look to what everyone else is doing but instead equip yourself with the knowledge and understanding that you need to do the job that you were called to do for such a time as this. You should be excited because even though you were not born queens and kings you will still die and inherit your fathers' mansion. My God how sweet is that.

Joseph in the bible went from a prison to a palace all because of the gift that God had given him. He hadn't studied at a college or planned to go from rags to riches but because God had given him a gift he was able to inherit more blessings than he ever imagined. Joseph was able to do more riding in the second chariot than most of you do riding in the first. I don't mind working under a leader because the work that I do isn't for man but is in fact for the one that made all man. Colossians 3:23 states: "Whatever you do, work at it with all your heart, as working for the Lord, and not man." We must learn that everything we do is for God. The problem isn't always that the leader isn't doing their job but the problem is often that we take focus off of God and place it on the leader that he has placed in charge. As loving and kind as God is, he is also a jealous God and will have nothing or no one placed before him. You are taking time away from God to talk about, and complain about a situation that you have no control over.

I myself question why some people are in charge. I have personally heard leaders gossip and backstab other leaders and half do their job. I have quit ministries in my mind very frequently because of foolishness and the lack of communication within the ministry but I was able to stand through it all without saying a word to man because I took everything to God in prayer. God is able to work it out. In fact he is so good that he works it out without any of your help. You have to keep your mind set on Jesus and do the works that he himself has called you to do. Now this can be very tricky to do if you are not in your set place. If you joined ministry because your friend is in the ministry or you like the people associated in it then you are in it for the wrong reason and you won't truly find peace. You have to seek God diligently so that he can place you in the right place and in the right position. Whether that place is leading the ministry or cleaning the bathroom stalls you work at it with all of your heart and soul, after all you aren't working for man but the great almighty, all powerful, everlasting God in heaven.

Now doesn't that make you want to ride in the second chariot? I know one thing and that is you can effectively be the best you can and get all of your blessings working only where God has placed you because your gift will always make room for you.

I was asked to teach a class regularly and agreed but started thinking in my mind that it wouldn't be an effective class because that class already had the exact amount of teachers needed. Instead of trying to figure it out I sat back and let God work it out. Surprisingly one of the teachers had been waiting patiently for another teacher to agree to teach so that he could teach a different class and be in his set place. My gift made room for me. I didn't have to argue, complain, or try to figure it out. All I had to do was stand still, give it to God and in his own way he worked it out.

Let God place you in your set place whether it is driving the car or sitting in the back seat, being a chief or an Indian. Humble yourself and work full-heartedly so that your blessings can flow accordingly. If God can take Joseph from a prison to a palace just sit back for a moment and think about what he can do for you. He is more than able and he is ready to bless you just where you are. If I were you I would stop complaining about riding in the second chariot and start thanking God in advance for having the power and authority to bless you in the position you are in. Get ready and prepare yourself for his overflow of blessings.

CHAPTER 8

Born to worship

You were not made to just be a doctor or lawyer. You were not made to be a housewife and raise a family nor were you made to sit on the front pew of your respected church. You and I were created to worship. With every breath in your body you should vow to worship God. Revelation 4:8 states, "Each of the four living creatures had six wings and was covered with eyes all around, even under his wings. Day and night they never stopped saying: "Holy, holy, holy is the Lord God Almighty, who was, and is, and is to come." They reverenced God because they knew who he was.

We sometimes don't reverence God because we don't know him personally. Yes you know that he died for your sins and yes you know a few scriptures, but when was the last time you spoke to God from your heart and waited for him to speak back to you? There is so much more to God than just saying the "Our Father" prayer and taking communion. God is worthy to be praised. He does more for you than you can even image. He watches over you when you sleep, wakes you up in the morning light, he is a light to your path, he makes your way easier, and comforts you when you need it the most. God is so amazing and so worthy to be praised but it is hard to worship an unknown God. You must learn to trust him and lean on his understanding.

I used to think something was wrong with calling on God throughout the day. But as I grew in Christ I learned that calling on the name of the Lord isn't a weakness in fact it is part of spiritual growth. When you call out the name of Jesus you are simply saying that you need his help and can't do it on your own. Let me call him for myself right now, Jesus, Jesus, Jesus. There is truly something about that name. At the mention of that name demons tremble, mountains move, situations have to change. There is healing, deliverance, and obedience in the name of Jesus. My God how sweet it is and what a privilege to call out his name. You will have to excuse me because I feel a holy-ghost two step praise dance coming on. In the words of my pastor, "Ain't he alright".

True worship is a lifestyle. When you truly worship it doesn't stop when the musicians stop playing or when the preacher gives the benediction. Worshipping becomes a part of who you are. When you worship God in spirit and in truth you are able to lose control of yourself and allow God to use you for his glory. Worship has to come from within. There should be a fire inside that burns within that moves on the outside. Worship doesn't have any particular day or hour in fact you should be able to worship any and every time your spirit moves you too.

Don't look at worship as something that you have to do but something that you choose to do. When you begin to worship you are able to connect with your father and he will tune in to what you have to tell him rather through song or prayer. I personally have a voice that only God wants to hear (trust me you would not want to hear me sing) But I am content with what I can't do because God has blessed me in a way that I am able to use the gifts that he has given me and worship him.

It isn't about being the best singer or strongest prayer warrior; it is about giving God your all from your heart. God knows when you are worshipping him for real and he faithfully honors your worship.

CHAPTER 9

When Jesus shows up

It doesn't matter who you are or what situation you are in, when Jesus shows up you better stop what you are doing and reverence the only one who is able to keep you from falling. I am reminded of the story in the book of Mark in the bible when Jesus entered a new city and a man by the name of Legion who was bonded by over two thousand demons kneeled down to Jesus and Jesus spoke and the demons fled from the man. This was a man who according to scriptures was in a tomb and even shackles couldn't hold him and chains were unable to keep him, yet when Jesus spoke the demons had no choice but to come out the man's body.

It is sad when demons fear Jesus yet Christians at times don't reverence him. You better wake up and realize who Jesus is. He is the great I Am. He is the alpha and omega. He is Jehovah. He is a father, a friend, a doctor, and a lawyer. He is a healer, a comforter, he is everything.

When Jesus shows up all is well. I was in worship service on Sunday morning and the atmosphere was simply amazing. It went from the talks of people greeting one another and laughing to a sweet aroma. It was as though Jesus himself was walking down every aisle and touching every pew. People were worshipping with hands lifted up and their mouths filled with praise. When Jesus shows up everything else is irrelevant. He has a way of making his presence known and I for one am so glad to know that my father in heaven thinks enough of me to show up in my life and make his presence known. Every knee shall bow and tongue shall confess that Jesus is Lord.

Can we stop and pause for a second and imagine what life would be like if Jesus had not shown up in our lives in the time that he had. I know you think you look good and you assume that you have everything figured out but don't get too big headed and forget where God has brought you from. You didn't always have the best of the best and if you are anything like me I would bet that you were not born with a silver spoon in your mouth. God did not have to send Jesus to die on our behalf in fact God didn't have to keep you in your right mind free from harm and danger, but he did. Had God not shown up you and I could have easily been homeless or living a life of a drug addict or prostitute. Most importantly we could easily be living in the land of the lost and dying. But God saw fit for one reason or another to show up in your lives. John 15:16 states: "You did not choose me, but I chose you, and appointed you to go and bear fruit-fruit that will last. Then the Father will give you whatever you ask in my name." The fruit is already inside of you, it is your right and responsibility to go out and live for God. He has already predestined you and ordered your steps. It is time that we not only carry the cross but follow the cross by any means necessary. I know you would like to imagine that you had something to do with all of this but the truth of the matter is you had nothing to do with where you are in your life. God choose you before you even knew who you were.

He placed the fruits of his spirit inside of you (love, joy, peace, self-control, gentleness, goodness, meekness, patience, faith) and anointed you to go out and do his good works.

The one thing that you must remember is that God is omnipresent. The word omnipresent is defined in the Webster New World dictionary as present in all places at the same time. In other words when you step in a room Jesus is there. When you leave the room, Jesus is there. He is everywhere at the same time waiting on you to show up. Even though there are times when he doesn't make his presence known he is still present. Twenty four hours a day, seven days a week, three hundred sixty-five days out of the year God is right here by your side. That can be a bit overwhelming to know that even when I don't realize he is present his spirit is still here. When I purposely sin he is watching. Even in the midnight hour when family and friends are gone God is right by your side. He is waiting if you need a shoulder to cry on, waiting when you need a friend to talk to. He is even waiting on you to repent of your wrongdoing and make a conscious decision to do what is right in his sight. What a might God we serve.

When God showed up in my life for the first time that I remember I was the young age of nine years old. I felt to my knees and started praying and I have not stopped yet. There is something that happens when I open my mouth and talk to God. He wraps his loving arms around me and holds me tight. He comforts me and lets me know that he sees me and hears all of my prayers. There is no prayer that I have ever prayed that God has not answered. He is real. I can testify because I know him for myself. I refuse to pray to an unknown God. I want the God that I pray to be there to talk with me and walk with me. I want him to show me the plans that he has for my life. I want him to be a mind regulator, heart fixer, and problem solver. I need him to make his presence known in my life and I thank him because he has made his presence known time and time again. He is great and so worthy to be praised.

CHAPTER 10

Don't get hung up on your mess ups

I can't join ministry. I will never find love because of my past. I am not good enough to sit on the front row. I just can't seem to get my life right; words of a typical sinner. Do you think that you are not the only one that messed up? Do you not know that we all have sinned and have fallen short of the glory of God?

Too often we get hung up on our mess ups. We sit and think of all the wrong that we have committed, the lies that we have told, and the scandals that we were involved in. We allow the guilt from our past to haunt us in the future and affect our tomorrows. Did you ever stop and think that God may have allowed you to go through all that you did for a reason. Did it not make you stronger? I am not in any way shape or form condoling wrongdoing but I am a firm believer that God is in control. And nothing and I do mean nothing can happen in your life or mine without him purposely allowing it to happen, which means that God saw you when you stole from your employer, he was right by your side when you lied to your spouse, he was even around when you fornicated with another person's significant other on last night yet he allowed you to commit the sin. Why? Because he knew that if and when you matured in him and spent time in his word daily you would refrain from the sin that is keeping you back. He knew that one day you would bow down before his throne and ask for forgiveness and walk in righteousness with him. The apostle Paul said it best in the book of Romans when he wrote in Romans 8:38: "For I am convinced that neither death nor life, neither angels nor demons, neither the present nor the future, nor any powers, neither height nor depth, nor anything else in all creation, will be able to separate us from the love of God that is in Christ Jesus our Lord."

You my friend must believe what the word of God says. You must be able to stand with the word when you have nothing and no one. You must be able to remind God of his promises and all that he has foretold you so that you don't let anything come between you and God. In other words don't get hung up on your daily mess ups.

Judas in the bible became hung up on his mess ups. He betrayed Jesus for thirty pieces of silver. He then felt so horrible for what he had done that he tried to give back the silver but when he saw that it was too late he beat himself up so much until he hung himself. Judas didn't understand that his betrayal had to happen in the way that it did and that God would have forgiven him of his sins if he simply asked. Judas like many of us allowed the voice of Satan to come into our minds and convince us that we are never going to get past that one incident and that we must give up and give in because it is too late for us to change. Well my friend today is your day. The good news is that there is no sin that our heavenly Father can not forgive. In fact the second you repent he forgives you and never brings up that sin again. Whether you stole a cookie from the cookie jar or committed multiple murders sin is sin and God forgives all.

The problem now is that you have not forgiven yourself. You have beaten up yourself over the sin you committed and don't know how to let it go. And because evil is ever present the enemy comes in and plays on your weak areas. He sees that you can't get past your shortcoming and failure so he does everything in his power to keep you down. In fact he beats you up when you are at your worst only to make you worse mentally and emotionally. Now you can't get mad at the enemy for doing his job because truth be told if you were focusing on God you wouldn't have time to see what that no good sneaky conniving devil was up too. You have to stay focused on God and remember that he has forgiven you and is waiting on you to move past your sin.

Once you move past your sin leave that sin in the past. Stop letting it get the best of you. You are better than that. In fact you are more than a conqueror. Being a conqueror means that you won a battle that you fought but you are actually more than a conqueror which means that you won a battle without even fighting. Let me pause right there so that you can get your praise on. You see you must understand that the battle is not yours and in fact the battle belongs to the Lord. And lucky for you the Lord has already fought and won the battle that you are trying to fight. This battle is not a physical battle but in fact it is a spiritual one. You must get your mind regulated and focus not on the things of this world but what is up above in heaven. For where your heart is that is also where you will find your treasure.

I pray that if anything is hindering you from doing the works you were called to do and living a life pleasing to God, it will seize. I pray that you will break free of bondages and release yourself of past hurt and pain. You have the power to move forward if and when you are ready to. You can do it but first you must believe in yourself and believe that the battle is already won.

CHAPTER 11

Who do you think you are?

You walk in church with your head held high. Dressed as though you are royalty, articulate, and carefree, who do you think you are? Let me tell you who I am I am a spirit filled, confident, bible talking, Jesus walking child of God.

There is absolutely nothing wrong with being confident in who you are and what you know about Christ. We need more bold Christians to stand up and not be afraid to tell somebody about the God that we serve. I know people are talking about you, so what. They talked about Jesus but that never stopped him from doing the work he was placed by God to do. People will talk about you until the day you die and there is absolutely nothing that you can do about it. In fact they will talk beyond the grave wondering why you wore what you did in the casket. Stop concerning yourself with what so called friends and family are saying about you. You have to be confident enough to stand up tall with your head held high and be the best you can be in the time that you have on this marvelous earth. Be you just as you were created to be. You don't have to like me that is fine. But I refuse to let anyone whether a man, woman, boy, girl, dog, cat, or demon stop me or block me from moving forward with the God that I serve.

That's right I said it and I stand behind what I say and mean it in every way. I am no longer ashamed to be who I am and nether should you. Do you not know, have you not heard? Jesus sacrificed his life for you to be able to live in his father's kingdom. I know it's overwhelming because you feel as though you don't deserve it but you are the heir of a king and it is time to start living as Christ intended for you to live.

I am not suggesting that you live outside of your weekly budget and throw away all of your clothes for fancy new threads nor am I saying that you have to sell your car and buy a new one or build a mansion on the other side of town but I am saying that it is time that you get the mind set of a child that is kingdom bound.

That simply means stop living as though God is not your father. He should be the one you call when your money is funny and change is strange, you should trust and depend on him and not the payday loan store across the street. God is the one that you should call in the midnight hour when you are lonely not the man next door who knows how to make you scream his name when he hits the right spot. God should be the one that you look to when your body is rocking with pain not the overpriced hospital who takes three hours to treat you. All of your help should come from God.

In order for your trust to come from God you have to know that he is able to see you through any and everything that you go through. That means you have to walk on water but instead of looking to the water look to the one who has the power to part a red sea. Look to God so that he can allow you to make it though those moments when it feels as though you can't go on any longer. Look to God when no one else is there to help you when you need it the most. Look to God everyday all day for the rest of your life.

Don't just look to God when things are going wrong. Learn to thank him when things are good so that through your storms you are able to sleep like a baby. Too often we look to God when we need one thing or another. We forget him when all our bills are paid and when there is money in our pocket but let hell break loose in any area of our lives and the first name we call on is Jesus. If you would take the time to get to know him like you should when things are going well you would be confident enough to trust him later when times are not as solid as you would like them to be.

Peter, a disciple from the bible was imprisoned and plans were made to stone him to death. The night before his arranged stoning Peter fell asleep with guards on the sides of him and chains on him. People outside were crying and praying for Peter but he slept peacefully. How is it that Peter was able to sleep at such a time? He was able to sleep because he knew that the battle was not his but the Lords'. He was able to sleep because he knew whether he slept on this side or the other side he would be sleeping with the Lord. Learn to sleep through your trials, sleep through your tribulations. But before you do I need you, in fact I dare you to put all of your trust in the almighty, all powerful, all knowing great God.

CHAPTER 12

I give myself away

I give myself away; what sweet words. I can feel chills running down my body every time I repeat those words; four simply yet powerful words. What an amazing feeling to be able to totally give yourself away. There is a release that must occur when you surrender to God. You must be able to give yourself to him freely and humbly. That simply means that you have to be willing to give him all of you and follow him completely.

Some of us, including myself struggle with giving ourselves away. We try and try but we can't seem to let go of doing what is pleasing us. But then there comes a time when we are tired of doing things on our own and tired of running in circles and we find ourselves having a "Jacob moment." Jacob, in the bible wrestled with God. In fact he told God that he would not let him go until he blessed him. So God did just that, he blessed him. But instead of blessing Jacob in a way that man would bless him God did something unusual. God took Jacob's hip bone and he broke it. The hip bone is in fact the strongest bone in your body. By God breaking Jacob's hip bone it forced Jacob to slow down and follow God.

You have to be careful of what you pray for and be even more careful of the manner in which you pray. Jacob, just like you and I wanted to be blessed. If I could imagine for a second I would imagine that Jacob had no idea that God was going to break his bone in order to bless him. But you must remember that in Isaiah 55:8 the bible states: "For my thoughts are not your thoughts, neither are your ways my ways", declares the Lord.' You, nor I, will never fully understand all of the ways of our heavenly father nor will we always agree with what he commands for us to do but if we trust him even when we can't trace him then we will be able to get to the place that he would have for us to go.

When we freely give ourselves away it is then that we are able to take off the mask that we have been hiding from for so long. Uncover the true you without caring who is looking. For too long we have been hiding because of tradition and different standards that this world has. It is time that we become free and let loose. There is a beautiful face under that mask and it is time that the world had a chance to see it. Whether that face is filled with freckles or beauty marks, scars or bruises it is time that we take off the mask and be free.

There is a woman that I look at every time I go downtown. She sits by the waterfall eating her snack. She isn't dressed in the finest clothes nor does she seem to possess any diamonds or riches. But she truly looks happy. She doesn't seem bothered that people are stopping to stare at her but instead she sits quietly and eats her snack without bothering a soul. That woman is free. She is confident enough in herself that she doesn't have to have a man by her side or friends in her corner. She sits alone day after day eating her snack away watching the water fall.

We have to stop consuming our selves with who is watching us and what people will say. I know some people sit and stare at me and others turn away and have unpleasant words to say. But to be frank I really don't care. I love the woman that I am and refuse to change for someone who has no power over the outcome of my days. I am free mind, body, and soul and I love it.

I dare you for just one day to completely and totally give yourself away. Forget about the crowd that you see everyday, forget about the co workers that gossip and snare. Forget about that man or woman who is all in your kool-aid and doesn't know the flavor. Let go just for one day. For twenty four hours let yourself be free. No worries, no fears, no doubts. Just be free.

CHAPTER 13

He says, she says, but what does God say?

Your significant other is sitting in the corner watching you get dressed and realizes that they do not like the outfit you chose to wear for dinner tonight. Even though you have spent five hours in a packed mall to find the right shoes to match the purse that goes perfectly with your outfit you decide to respect your significant others' opinion and you go to the closet spend fifteen minutes deciding what to change into then spend another half hour getting your hair and make up right. You finally make it to dinner and the couple that you are meeting with for dinner tells you that you look very classy but your outfit doesn't go well with the place you chose to have dinner at. You get home and soak in a hot tub upset because you feel as though your entire night was ruined. The next morning you get a call from a member of your church informing you that the bulletin you put up in the hallway is offensive towards others and the church has been getting complains since it was put up. They need you to immediately make it to the church and take down your bulletin. On your way there you realize that you had a missed call from your boss who is furious because he doesn't agree with the work that you turned in and even though you know what you did was authentic and original you don't have the courage to stand up to him so you decide to spend five hours redoing your work after hours just to please your boss. Everyone in your life seems to have something to say. My question is what does God say?

We seem to value everyone's opinion but when it comes to checking in with God we seem to have selective amnesia. You know what selective amnesia is, it is when you pick and chose exactly what it is that you want to remember. We all have it at times. In fact I think I just experienced it a few days ago when the bill collector called me unexpectedly.

We as Christians have to remember that God always has the final say. In fact his say is the only one that should matter because he always knows what is best for his children. He is the leading Sheppard and we are the helpless sheep in need of direction and guidance. When we pray to God he listens to what we have to say and when God speaks to us we should humbly tune in to what he has to say. He miraculously is able to speak to all of his children in ways that we are able to comprehend. God speaks to some through dreams and others through song. He knows exactly how to get through to all of his sheep in a manner in which we understand. I have heard the voice of God more times than I can count. God has even spoken to me through dreams and through other people. He has always come to me in ways that I can understand and because of him talking to me I am able to follow accordingly.

God will never lead us astray but one thing is for sure and that is that unfortunately God's voice isn't the only voice that we hear. You are so wrapped up in your own world that you can't discern the voice of God from that of the enemy. So you wander aimlessly like the Israelites hoping that you will find your way back. The only problem is the more you wander off the further you get from being able to positively discern the voice of God.

God speaks in a quiet still voice. Neither his voice, nor his intend is never to frighten you but to guide you along your path in life. He wants all of his children to listen and more importantly follow when he calls.

If you have not yet tapped into hearing God on a daily basis I would like to challenge you to get away from the hustle and bustle of your everyday life and go to your secret closet and wait patiently for God to speak.

It saddens me when people are in tune to what man says but are not able to recognize the voice of their father in heaven. The reason you know your mothers voice and the voice of your co worker is because you have spent time with that person and now realize the sound of their voice. Just like you spend time with family and friends you my friend, need to set aside some time throughout your day and spend it with the Lord.

CHAPTER 14

No More Excuses

I wanted to attend Sunday school but, I was about to start reading the bible but, you know I am going to lead a new ministry but. We are so full of excuses. What if God gave us excuses? What if he said I was going to bless you today but or I thought about waking you up this morning but. If God was like man none of us would still be alive today. We make excuse for every reason under the sun. If we don't feel like doing something or can't seem to have things go our way we find an excuse. An excuse my friend is just your justification of why you don't do what you should. Just in case you didn't quite get what I just said let me be kind enough to repeat it for you. An excuse is your justification of why you don't do what you should. That's right I said it and to be honest I mean just what I said.

Break free from making excuses. You are limiting what you can do by picking and choosing what you want to do. We have to learn to get out of our comfort zone and man up (may not be proper English but you and I both know that it is the truth). Go out and do it even though you have never done it before, stop being afraid. And for you who are sitting back saying you have no fear well what exactly is stopping you? Are you lazy? Do you like sitting on your backside all day long watching television and playing hand held games. Why are you not getting busy in your neighborhood and going out in the community helping under privileged children or going to your local church and helping organized items for the outreach ministry? While Jesus was speaking to the disciples he stated in Mark 10:43: "Not so with you. Instead, whoever wants to be great among you must be your servant." It doesn't say you have to be a doctor or lawyer, evangelist or preacher, nurse or paramedic. It doesn't even say you have to be a singer or entertainer, rich nor famous. The bible says whoever wants to be great must become a servant. Wow, doesn't that excite you? Knowing that all you have to do is go out and be a servant of the Lord and you too shall be great. That is music to my ears. The words servant of the Lord makes me want to dance. Hold my coat for a little while so I can take a break and have a holy-ghost two step.

Whether you are the person that directs the choir or the one that is assigned to mop the floor, you need to be the best servant of the Lord that you possible can. Walk with your head held high and chest poking out because you are doing the work of your heavenly father. I want to be great. I want to do great things, what exactly the Lord has in store for me I don't know but what I do know is that I have made up my mind and decided in my heart that I am going to no longer make excuses. I am going to be about my Father's business and I am going to go out and serve the church, serve my community, and serve my country in any way that I possible can. Someone has to make a change, why not let that change begin with you.

Everyone can not do everything but I guarantee you that we all can do something. We need to change our minds from I don't want, to Lord what do you want. It is time that we walk like Jesus and talk like Jesus. It's time that we be the servants of Christ that we were called to be. No more waiting on our neighbor to get the job done we can go out and with the grace and mercy of God we can get the job done ourselves. We are the head and not the tails, the lender and not the borrower. We are more than conquerors. No more excuses men and women of God we need to get it together. You can't help get my house in order until you clean up yours. So right now start cleaning. Take out all of the excuses that you once had, put it in a black garbage bag, walk out to the dumpster and throw it away. After all today is the first day of the best day of the rest of your very blessed lives.

CHAPTER 15

Sweep around Your own Front Door before You Try Sweeping around Mine

Excuse my language but how in the hell do you find the nerve to come to my house trying to clean it when you are living in a pig pen. One of my biggest pet peeves is when a person who knows they have skeletons in their closet will come around me acting holier than thou and have the nerve to tell me how to live my life. I have four little words for you: TAKE OFF THE MASK! Who do you think you are fooling? Are you in my business so I don't get in yours? Or maybe you want to be involved in my life because you haven't surrendered yourself and you feel as though you have no life of your own. Whatever the reason may be you need to look deep inside yourself and find out what is causing you to be the way that you are. No one wants to be around a control freak who tries to control other people because they have no control over their own lives.

What nerve they have telling me how I should live my life, and whom I should and shouldn't date. Some even walk around saying "Oh I wouldn't do that if I were you." Newsflash you are not me! You will never be me, you don't have to talk to me and you don't have to concern your nosy self with me. There are two types of people; there are those that are nosy and those that observe. What is the difference? I am so glad that you asked. Sit back, relax, and let me explain the difference to you. A nosy person will be entirely in your business but will refuse to tell you any of their business. A nosy person wants to know where you are going, who you have been with, how much money you have, who you are sleeping with, etc. But when you question them they shut down like a car with no gas. They don't want you to know any of their business but they are all in yours wishing you would tell them what goes on in your life so that they can go and spread your business like a wild fire. Then there are those that observe. A person that observes will ask you nothing yet already knows everything. They see you when you don't even notice them and they watch your mannerisms. They observe the types of people you hang out with and the conversation that you have. They know the type of car you drive and some even know what neighborhood you live in. They know all this not from asking you and not from you telling them. They know because they have observed you. You can ask them questions about their life and they will tell you without questioning you about yours, why, because they have seen for themselves who you are without asking you a single question.

I actually have more respect for those that observe you than those that are just plain nosy. If you took time to observe me than there is obviously something that I have that you want that you wish you had. Did I lose you I hope not. You see an observant person has enough respect to allow you to show who you are through your actions than your words. The ones that observe are usually not the ones that are back stabbing you and gossiping behind your back. In fact observers usually are the quietest ones in the room.

They sit back and take it all in while the nosy ones go from table to table trying to find out the latest gossip.

I do not know whether you consider yourself to be nosy, I hope not, or observant but either way please don't be that person that people run from because you are always in everyone's business. Instead why don't you take a good long look in the mirror and get to know who you truly are and let go of the pride that is holding you back. Thoroughly clean up your own house and respect me enough by allowing me to clean my own. If God wanted you in charge of me he would have made you my keeper instead he made you my sister/brother in Christ so that when I do need help cleaning my house you can assist me rather than take over.

Take some time and clean your house. Get your business in order, because you can't help me put my make up on if you yourself are in need of a make over.

CHAPTER 16

Be About your Father's Business

You mind everyone else's business why not mind the business of your father? I know that was a little harsh but you and I both know that it is the truth. The truth may not always be what you want to hear but trust me it is always needed and if done in the right manner it will be appreciated.

In the New Testament, the book of Luke chapter three speaks about how Jesus and his parents went to Jerusalem for the Feast of the Passover. When it was time to leave Jesus' parents left assuming he was with them but after traveling for a day it was noticed that Jesus was not there. They searched for him among family and friends but were unable to find him. After three days they found him in the temple courts sitting among the teachers asking questions. His parents questioned why he treated them as he did as they had been searching for him for three days. Jesus answered by saying he had to be in his father's house.

Jesus knew that he had to be about his fathers' business. He knew that he had to be where his father was in order to understand the business of his father. One reason we don't get the blessings we should is because we are not in the position to receive the blessings. You can't ask God to bless you but refuse to position yourself accordingly.

1 Kings 19:11 states: 'The Lord said, "Go out and stand on the mountain in the presence of the Lord, for the Lord is about to pass by." In other words where you are standing isn't where you need to be. You need to position yourself so that you can be where the blessings are so that you can get all that God has for you. You wonder why you still do not possess an answer to your prayers; it may be because you haven't moved from the spot you were standing in on the day that you prayed. I know you sit in the same seat every Sunday in church waiting for a fresh anointing to fall fresh on you, but it may be that you have been sitting in that seat for far too long and you need to move to a new seat. You have to get in the position to receive your blessings.

One way to position ourselves is to be about our fathers' business. How do we do that? Take a few minutes, sit back and relax while I explain it. When you are about your fathers' business you do as you father instructs. You forsake all others and you focus on the business of your father. His business is to get his people saved. His business is to help people get closer to him. His business is to show people who he is so that he can be reverenced. His business is to give his children an eternity of peace and happiness.

Being about your fathers' business is not always the easiest thing to do. In fact it can be one of the hardest. You have to literally deny yourself and follow your father. In fact the scripture tells us that if a man is on his honeymoon he is to leave his wife to follow the Lord. In other words you must always be willing to go if and when needed.

As loving and kind as our father in heaven is, he is also a jealous God and will have nothing and no one before him. You have to be willing to put him first. First means he is to go before that man or woman you lay with every night and before that child that you tuck in for bed. God is to be first, no exceptions.

To be honest God deserves to be first. You need to understand just who he is because putting a God who you don't know first may be nearly impossible. God is the one who took nothing and turned it into something. He spoke light where there was darkness. God said to let there be expanse between the waters to separate water from water and it was so. God said to let the land produce vegetation: seed bearing plants and trees on the land that bear fruit with seed in it, according to their various kinds, and it was so. God said to let the water under the sky be gathered to one place and let dry ground appear and it was so. God took a rib from a man and made a woman, in which woman is able to create all beings through the power and wonders of God.

It is time that we all took the time to really get to know our creator. All too often we walk around making excuses for the way that we live saying statements like, "God knows my heart" and "I'm saved so I am going to heaven I don't need to read the bible". We will each be accountable for our own actions. We must be willing to dig deeper into who we are and our creator's promises that he made unto us.

I don't know about you but I refuse to wait until I die to get some heaven, I want heaven on earth and by faith I shall inherit it. You are the master of your mind and it is you who will get you to the next level of your life. You have to believe that God is able to give you everything that you have every wanted and asked him for. But I suggest that while you are waiting on your heaven on earth you get your life in order because to tell you the truth the God that I serve don't bless no mess! Now I know that may not be proper English but it is truthful. You can't walk around living a life of purposeful sin then expect God to give you all that you ask for just because you are saved. Salvation promises eternal life with God. Living a life dedicated to God promises answered prayers and a close connection to God.

Don't wait until you die to enjoy an eternity of peace. God is willing to give you peace right where you are. He wants all of his children to enjoy the earth that he made with his own hands. You have more power than you realize. You have the power to make sound decisions and the power to be about your Fathers' business.

CHAPTER 17

True Fasting

What a feeling you get when you fast. Fasting isn't about losing weight or focusing on what you can and can't eat. When you fast it isn't a way to manipulate God into giving you what you have been asking for. True fasting is your way of sacrificing what hinders you from getting to God. When you fast it is personal. You are fasting so that you can get closer to God. James 4:8 states: "Come near to God and he will come near to you. Wash your hands, you sinners, and purify your hearts, you double-minded."

I was dealing with a situation and could not see my way out. I decided to fast from all foods for seven days or until God answered my prayers. The first day of fasting I sought God but never heard his voice. The second day I waited and prayed but again I heard nothing. By the third day I just knew that I would hear God, after all I hear the voice of God daily so I was positive that he would answer my prayers yet God did not respond. The third day came and went yet still no words from God. By the fourth day I was getting impatient and tired and by that night since I had still not heard from God I gave in and ate. I didn't eat because I was hungry but instead I ate because I was upset and disappointed that the same God whose voice I hear daily had chosen not to speak to me when I needed to hear from him the most. After eating I felt horrible and I repented. I knew it was wrong to give in like I did so I decided to start my fasting over because I had enough faith in God and I knew that even though he didn't come when I wanted, I believed that he would come on time. The next day I was spiritually ready and I decided to restart my fast. I went to noon day prayer as I usually did and in the balcony while I was praying for the church God began to speak to me. He didn't speak to me about the church but instead he began speaking to me about everything that I had been praying for throughout my fasting. My God how great is our God.

Even though I am faithless God is still faithful. He still came through. God doesn't move when we tell him too, he moves when he is ready. I know you have been seeking him, keep seeking him. He will come through for you. I am a living witness that though he may not come when I want him he is always on time. He is a good God who is thankfully the one sure thing in my life and in yours.

He is real and he is ready for you to seek him through true fasting and praying.

There are some situations that may only change through fasting and praying. Don't get it twisted fasting isn't a way to manipulate God. He isn't a genie in a bottle that will move just because you choose to fast. When you fast it is personal. Fasting is your time to take away anything that may hinder you from getting to God. With so many distractions like food, people, music, technology, and extra curriculum activities is very easy to stray away. Fasting keeps us connected. It allows us to refocus on what matters the most. Do not spend time focusing on what you are giving up when you fast but instead focus on who you are getting closer too; focus on Jesus.

CHAPTER 18

You are not fooling anyone but yourself

He sits on the pulpit every Sunday with hands lifted up. She sings as beautiful as a hummingbird and can hold a note longer than your favorite gospel artist. Yet when he steps down from the pulpit he gets in his car and drives to the local convenient store and buys a bottle of gin and two packs of condoms. The woman who just sang praises to God has finished her last song and left the church. She goes to her house and waits patiently for her company. There is a knock at the door. Who could it be? It is none other than the man from the pulpit with his gin in his left hand and his condoms in his right. The woman excitedly welcomes him into her bedroom and he closes the door behind. One hour later he walks out of the room, familiar with the house he sees his way out. He goes home to his wife and children while the woman he just had consensual sex with washes up before her husband comes home. Both the man from the pulpit and the woman who sang songs of praise in the church live their lives as though they are living a life pleasing to God when the whole time they are doing nothing more than simply fooling themselves.

Maybe your wife will never found out that you committed adultery and your husband may never realize that the child that calls him daddy isn't his. Your boss may never realize how much money you stole from the business and your church congregation won't see that you are nothing but a hypocrite. But the fact of the matter, whether anyone finds out what wrong you do or not, you are not fooling anyone but yourself. God saw you this morning and watched you late last night. You have to find out who you are and what you want for yourself out of this life. There is no one who can give you happiness or put a smile on your face. You have to look deep within your soul and get to know who you are. It is when you know who you are that you are able to live a life acceptable and pleasing to God and to yourself.

Purposeful sin will only bring you happiness for so long. It may feel good today but what about tomorrow? There will come a time in your life when you will realize that you have missed out because of foolishness sin.

You cannot change your past. The events are already done and you don't have the power to change it. There isn't a need to beat yourself over the past or cry about what you feel you should have did better. You and only you control the decisions that you make from now on. Right now you can make a conscious decision to live a life that will give you true joy and peace.

I was once at a place in life where I thought that I could make it straddling the fence. I figured that because I didn't know many people at the time and I hadn't fully committed myself to live a life pleasing to God I could do anything I wanted. And while I felt good at the time I must be honest and tell you that I felt horrible with the decisions that I had made. I wanted more for myself and so should you. You are a queen or king and you need to conduct yourself accordingly.

Don't feed into your flesh. One reason that we do wrong is because we are hungry. When you are hungry you will eat any and everything whether you want it or not. It's like a married man who has a wonderful wife at home but he goes out and commits adultery with a prostitute. It may not be because he wanted to be involved with someone else, but it may be that he was not getting what he wanted at home and felt as though he had to get it elsewhere, in other words he was hungry. Matthew 4:4 states: "Jesus answered, "It is written: 'Man does not live by bread alone, but on every word that comes from the mouth of God." When we are hungry for food we eat. We rush to a fast food restaurant or the nearest burger joint. It doesn't matter what the cost or how long the wait we will do whatever we have to so that we eat until we are full. Fortunately for Christians there is a different type of food. It is spiritual food and we must learn to fill up on it so that we do not go hungry. A hungry man will eat from the garbage can but a man that is full when he leaves his house will have no want for anything else. The reason we fall for so much foolishness outside our homes is because we didn't take the time to get full before we left our homes.

It is time to get full. There are sixty-six books waiting to fill your spirit. You can start from when Jesus took two fish and five loaves of bread and fed five thousand than you can read about how Jesus calmed the storm. From Genesis to Revelation you can fill your spirit in a way that you will never go hungry again.

CHAPTER 19

Falling in Love with Jesus

I was asked the question; "Is there a difference between loving someone and being in love with someone" My response was, yes. When you love someone you genuinely care about that person. You want the best for them and you have a respect for them. When you are in love, your feelings change in a way that you want to be around the person and get to know them in every way. You observe them and do whatever it takes to put a smile on their face. When in love you make the choice to forsake all others just to be with that one special person that brightens your day and makes you tingle all over.

When I fell in love for the first time, unfortunately it wasn't with Jesus. I have always loved the Lord and had respect for his word, but it took me years to fall in love with him. In fact it wasn't until I fully surrendered myself to him that I was able to understand just who he was and how wonderful being in his presence is. I began to get more in the word and focused on finding out all there was to know about the love of my life. And the more I studied and prayed the more he would make his self known in my life.

I went from reading the bible, to living the word. In other words I now practice what I preach. I have a new love for the word and most importantly for my heavenly father. My prayer went from Lord I love you to Lord I desire to fall in love with you more and more each day.

There is truly something about the name Jesus. My soul gets happy, my heart beats faster, my mind is regulated and I am at peace. You must make the choice to fall in love with Jesus and all that he stands for. Like any relationship you will get upset and sometimes feel like all of the work that you do is in vein but if you just keep the faith I promise you that you will receive all of the benefits of being a Christian. Galatians 6:9 states: "And let us not be weary in well doing: for in due season we shall reap, if we faint not." Everything in your life will happen accordingly. Your season of weeping will come but you have to trust God and hold tight to his unchanging hand.

Man's love will give earthly benefits but God's love gives you eternal benefits like a heaven to rest your head for an eternity.

Falling in love with Jesus is easier said than done. Why, because you cannot wear a mask. If you are a woman you can't layer your face with make-up and hide behind foundation, men you can't let your beard grow out and assume that God can't see past it. After all you know what happens when you make an assumption don't you.

God will not force you to fall in love, like some men. Instead you are allowed to make a conscious decision. Falling in love means you must be willing to sacrifice. You can't straddle the fence nor can you play on the sideline. You have to be willing to get in the game and play even if it means going into overtime.

We can't run nor can we hide from God. He is everywhere and he knows our heart. If you are longing for a closeness to your Father and you desire to give yourself away to him than may I suggest that you take a good look in the mirror and look past the outer man and look deep into the inner man and find out what is stopping you from giving your all to God. For most people it is a fear of what others will say and think about them. Let me tell you something unless man or woman has the power to wake you each morning and put you back to sleep each night stop allowing them to dictate who you are and the person you were designed to become.

Falling in love with Jesus was by far the very best thing that I have ever done. When I am lonely he wraps his loving arm around me. When I am upset he comforts me. When I am confused he regulates my mind. He has given me true peace that surpasses all human understanding. My prayer is that I don't ever fall out of love.

It is very easy to fall out of love. When we stray away from God and his word it causes us to move away from him. There are many daily distractions from television and music to drugs and alcohol. That is why you must stay connected whether through bible study or daily personal talks with God you have to find time to stay connected.

It's easy to stay connected when you are committed. But staying committed does mean that you will have to sacrifice. Whether it's time with family and friends or deciding whether to pick up an extra shift at work you have to find time to spend with God.

Spending time doesn't mean that your life will be perfect, because trust me it will not. But it will definitely help you be able to overcome the daily temptations of life and sleep through your storms. Besides you can be in church twenty-three hours in a day but it is that one hour that you step out that the enemy will come after you. Take heed, because if you spend time with the Lord and you trust that the Lord lives inside of you and you know that the enemy is not stronger than the Lord than you know that there is absolutely nothing that the enemy can do to you.

Relax because you have the Lord on your side. Don't just take what you read and believe it; I dare you to fall in love with Jesus for yourself. It will truly be the best thing that you have ever done.

CHAPTER 20

Be Careful what you ask for because you just may get it

Oh my gosh, there was this tall attractive man I noticed in the neighborhood and every time I saw him he was spending time with all of his children. When I passed him in the park, he was there with his children, when we bypassed in the grocery store he was walking down the aisle looking for different food that his children liked. I even heard him talk with another male and of course his conversation was about how a joy it is to have children and how he has dedicated his life to tending to them and making them happy. I made the comment in my mind, Lord why can't you send me a man like that. Approximately one week later I saw this man again. He walked up to me, introduced his self, and ironically asked for a chance to get to know me better. My first thought was, wow God heard my prayer. So of course we exchanged telephone numbers.

You know I was thinking everything would be all good, after all the bible says if we ask we shall receive. So I went home and later that night we began communicating. We actually started getting to know each other via text and then after a week or two he called. Oh my goodness, what in the world did I get myself into. Excuse me but that fool was crazy. Immediately after speaking with him I said Lord, please take him out of my life, this isn't what I want.

That was one of the moments that I knew that God hears all and he answers accordingly. He heard my prayer when I asked for that man and even though God knew that he was not for me in any way, shape, or form God still allowed me to see for myself instead of wondering what could have or should have been.

You better be careful what you pray for because you just may get it. Not everything that glitters is gold and trust me when I say that the grass isn't always greener on the other side. In fact when you look over at the grass on the other side there is nothing but weeds and dirt.

There is a valuable lesson that I learned from the incident with the man that I asked for. That lesson is to seek God for what he has for you rather than asking for what you think that you want. God's plan for your life is always better than any other plans that you can think or imagine for yourself. You have to diligently seek God and be receptive to what he tells you. When he says wait; you wait. When he says no; respect it. When he says go; you better move. God is in control and he knows you better than you could possible know yourself.

We unfortunately force things to work in our favor. You force yourself into a new position at work but now you cannot seem to understand how to carry your workload efficiently. You decided to force yourself with the man you are physically attracted to but now you realize you don't have any true feelings for him. You even forced yourself into a new car because everyone else has one now you are at home pulling your hair out wondering how you will be able to afford to pay your monthly note. When you force situations in your life to happen they seem to happen somehow but they never last the entire time because those things were never truly meant for you.

The bible does say that if you ask you shall receive but you must remember that if you receive anything outside of God's will for your life you will not be truly happy nor will you appreciate what God has purposely predestined for you.

CHAPTER 21

God is not the Author of Confusion

God is never the author of confusion but as sad as it is to say, we are. Not that it is intentional but we sometimes cause confusion in our homes, jobs, and yes even at church. One way we cause confusion is by moving ahead of God. You feel that something should be done about a situation so you in your own power and mite take it upon yourself to go and handle the situation. The only problem is, you can't. In fact all you will do is cause confusion and cachos because you were led by your flesh and not that of the Holy Spirit.

It is human nature to want to step in and take control of a situation, especially when God seems to be no where around. But you have to learn that you must take everything, and I do mean everything to God in prayer and leave it there. There is no taking it back. You have to totally let the situation go because in his hands all is well.

There are different ministries that I know I was called to be part of. In my mind I have quit one of those ministries regularly. Every time I think of what goes on in that ministry and the lack of the holy spirit flowing I get upset to my stomach and make a personal vow never to return to that ministry again. Yet every month I attend the meeting. Why? Because I didn't put myself there and I can't force myself to leave. When God places you in a particular place it's not to cause confusion nor is it for you to feel uneasy or even for you to have a want to quit. It is for you to focus on him.

It's hard to focus on God when there are distractions in the ministry. But the harder the distractions, the more focused you need to be on God. He is purposely allowing certain situations to come in your life. Truth be told if you were totally focused on God and not which deacon is accused of sleeping with the usher you wouldn't have time to worry yourself with things of this world. The bible tells us that where our heart is that is where our treasure is also. I have made up my mind to fix my heart on heaven and its' wonderful glory.

It seems at times that the church is merely a playground for people. They come when they want to relax and leave after they have played. They don't stay long enough for class to be in session instead they fit the church into their schedule. Then they sit and wonder why there is so much confusion.

Do you want to know why confusion is all around the church? One word: Communication. People are to fearful of what someone will think of them if they tell them what's on their mind. Others are too scared to communicate their true feelings about an idea or changes in the church so they sit back let it build up then they explode or leave the church. They don't leave because they have been led to another church but they leave because there is no communication in the church that they are affiliated with.

Communication is powerful. In fact it is all that we have. Communication is how we speak to God and how God speaks to us. Without communication there is self delusion, confusion, and assumptions. We have to be able to speak out. If that means taking a step back from the situation to see it more clearly than do that. One of the reasons we don't effectively communicate is because we are too close to the problem. You hang out with the person causing the problem, you know their families, and you don't want to risk losing the friendship that you worked so hard to build. So you don't communicate thinking things will get better but they only get worse.

Are you scared that the person will end your friendship? If so good, let them go. They were probably hindering your walk anyway. And I don't know about you but there is no one, man or woman, young or old, black or white, rich or poor, that will hinder my walk or block my blessings from God.

Learn how to effectively communicate. I am not talking about back slander and gossip I am taking about respecting the person enough to tell them what's right and what's wrong. I have lost so called friends behind the lack of communication. It's one thing when you lose someone at work or a friend that you hang out with. But to lose someone that you attend church with and are in ministry with over lack of communication; that is simply horrible.

I know it hurts to lose people in ministry because I lost someone in ministry over a lack of communication. This person and I met and were starting to become friends. We spoke frequently and she even hung out with my family and I during a gathering. A few months past and she became involved with a man that was a mutual friend. They courted for a few months and then dated for a few days before the relationship was over. Now let me make it clear by saying the fact that the relationship ended had absolutely nothing to do with me, yet for some reason under the sun the female along with her friends assumed that I was the reason. I would walk in church and hear them smirking about me and what they assumed occurred. They would roll their eyes when I walked pass them. They even would say fake hellos and good byes before and after meetings. All she had to do was communicate and it would end all assumptions but instead she walked around "assuming" something that never was. I tried talking to her a few times about the situation but it was never allowed. It wasn't until a year and a half later when I saw her in the grocery store that she spoke. Of course she didn't speak of the situation, neither did I, but there was something different when she spoke. She seemed real. Afterwards she reached out and hugged me, we then said our good byes, and walked away. Now I don't know if she spoke and seemingly was over the situation because she has a new boyfriend or what the reason was, but there was definitely something different about being in her presence this time then there was before. Were this girl and I ever going to be best friends had this incident not occurred, of course not. But the fact that a situation of this sort was able to cause confusion because of a lack of communication, that saddens me.

I will be honest it hurt to know that a person would rather lose my friendship than communicate with me but I am glad that it happened because I don't want a friend like that. I want someone who loves and cares about me enough to tell me the truth and respectfully communicate with me at all times.

We must learn how to talk, when to talk, and in the appropriate manner in which to talk. Communication is all we have. I pray that you use it accordingly.

CHAPTER 22

When did I become this person?

From partying and smoking black and mind cigars to using profanity toward everyone that told me something I didn't like; I have truly changed. I can't recall one particular event that happened that caused me to make such a drastic change but along the way I have truly changed. I sometimes have to take a step back and take it all in. I am not saying that I am perfect because I am not nor will I ever be, but I can honestly and whole heartedly confess that I have truly changed.

The same music doesn't excite me. I don't feel the need to listen when people are gossiping around me. I don't have a want to go out and party or sleep around before marriage. It is like a total transformation has occurred in my life and I do not feel as though I deserve it. I was on a fast slope to hell doing any and everything that I pleased. Disregarding the consequences of my actions and not caring about those I may have hurt in the process. But God saw fit to not only allow me to live to see another day, but he saw fit to save me, deliver me, and set me free of strongholds and bondages. I will never be worthy nor will I ever fully understand why he loves me but I do know one thing for sure and that is that I have been changed by the unfailing power of the almighty God.

Change never occurs over night. There is no magic potion you can take to be cured and fully delivered. There is a process that must first occur. For one you must take off the mask. You have pretended to be someone that you are not for too long. You have laughed at jokes that offended you and hung out with people who have purposely tried to harm you. It is now time for the real you to come out. Be unique. People will like and respect you for who you are and if they don't I suggest that you humbly let them go.

Once your mask is off you need to take a good long look in the mirror and find out who you truly are. Look at what you love about yourself and for the things you don't like be bold enough to change it and for what you can't change, you must humbly accept.

Then you must seek God's guidance. Ask him to show you who you were created to be and ask him to order your steps in his word. It will take lots of patience on your part because God doesn't always come in the time or fashion that we would like him to. Instead he takes the time and he helps builds your character and strengthens your areas of weakness.

I know you think that you are ready for God to change you, and who knows you may be. But there is a difference from being ready and being fully prepared. Being ready means you are available. Which simply means you can go when called. But being prepared means not only are you ready but you can take whatever comes your way and stand through the trials and tribulations of life because you have fully allowed God to take his time and prepare you into the person he ordained and predestined you to become.

I have come to the realization that everyday is a day of recommitting unto the Lord. You must recommit yourself daily. And most importantly you must crucify your flesh. Your flesh wants what it wants but you have to be strong enough in your spirit to crucify your flesh and follow the sprit of the Lord.

CHAPTER 23

Embrace the new you

It is awesome when other people love the person that you have become but it is truly inspiring when you are able to love and embrace the person you are from within. I dare you to embrace who you are. I want you to take some personal time alone and get to know who you have become and fall in love with yourself. Too often we expect others to love what we ourselves don't love and appreciate.

When you embrace yourself you will be able to change what you do not like and accept what you can not change. Embracing yourself is more than just spending quiet time alone or reading a good book. When you truly embrace yourself you are able to look within your soul and find out the person in which you truly are.

I am six feet tall with freckles on my face and I love it. I am kind hearted and I have a deep love for the word of God. I am also impatient at times and like to be left alone. I have embraced who I am and I am working toward being the woman of God that I was created to be.

There is no woman or man who can define who you are. Neither is there a person on God's beautiful green earth that can change you, after all you can't change what you didn't create. Only God can change you but you have to be a willing participate.

I still to this day don't understand how people can think that with the right love and affection they can change someone. Some think if they do everything perfectly the person will miraculously change while others assume that change will occur naturally with age. For the sake of argument let's say that you can change someone. You are with them and after ten years they change into the person that you have always wanted them to be. They are now more considerate and loving and they are living a life pleasing to God. In fact they now seem like the perfect person. Do you really think after they change they will still want to be around you? After all they will be renewed and refreshed and may want someone new. You have to be careful of what you pray for and even more careful of the manner in which you pray.

Embracing oneself must come from within each individual. I can't change you nor can you change me but we can pray that God will work his way into our hearts and give us each the desire to change in a way that is pleasing to him.

Leave the old no good, gossip talking, no faith walking person in the past and embrace the beautiful person that you were created to be. Embrace the new you.

CHAPTER 24

Fall in love with who you are

I am fearfully and wonderfully made. From the crown of my head to the soles of my feet I love who I am and the person that I am becoming.

You have to love yourself. What you don't like; change. What you can't change; accept. There will never be another like you. When God created you he went into his secret place and made you. It is no accident that you are the skin tone that you are nor is it coincident that you are a certain height. God loves you just as you are yet that love will be hard to accept if you don't love who you are.

For a moment I want you to forget about the model on television or that perfectly portioned individual next to you. Stop looking at what another possess and look to what makes you unique. We often focus on what we don't have and forget to be thankful for what we do have and who we are. There is someone somewhere wishing they had your beauty and possessed your self confidence. There is a woman with no legs who wishes to walk again while you are sitting at home complaining because you feel your legs are too big. There is a cancer patient who has lost all of the hair on their head and would give anything to be able to have hair like yours yet you have the nerve to sit at home and miss out on life because you are having a bad hair day.

Learn to love yourself. Start with loving who you are on the inside. What are all of the characteristic traits that you posses and where is the amazing heart that God has given you? You must find out who you truly are.

One of my daily prayers is that God allows me to fall in love with him more and more each day. But if I can be honest I must admit that I didn't fully fall in love with him until I fell in love with myself. I had to take time to find out what makes me smile and how to accept what I could not change.

If you don't love you then how on earth do you expect others to love you? True beauty and self worth comes from within. There is something amazing when I see a self confident Christian who not only loves the Lord but they indeed truly love themselves. I am not at all saying for you to be conceited, for if anyone thinks he is something when he is not he is deceiving himself, but I am saying that you do have to love yourself and fall in love with who you are.

I would imagine that it saddens God to know that some do not love and respect the person that he himself has purposely made them to be. He could have hand-made you to become anyone yet he perfectly chose you to be just as you are. You must gracefully accept it and embrace who you have become.

Every one of us at some point or another, searches for a hero not fully understanding that we have a hero that lives inside of each of us. You need to make the decision not to walk in anyone's shadow instead walk in the grace and mercy that God has gracefully provided for each of his wonderful children.

CHAPTER 25

Accept others for who they have become

When we initially meet people we assume that the manner in which we met them will remain the same. But in most cases that is not what happens. Have you ever heard anyone say "we have outgrown one another?" That term is used when two people have been connected with each other for an ample amount of time yet one or both of the individuals seem to have grown intellectually leaving the other individual in the same mental state that they were when the friendship/relationship first began.

We all start off as babies however there is not any individual that remains the way they were the first day they were born. In fact during the first year there is an amazing growth that takes place. Babies learn to crawl, walk, eat age appropriate food, make noises and sounds, and their physical feature as well as their mental state grows.

Just as a baby changes you should also change. You should be more mature today than you were on yesterday. You shouldn't make the same mistakes and use the same excuses. In other words you have to get off of the formula. You wouldn't dare see a forty year old man sit at his desk at work sucking a pacifier. We all must go through change and when we do we must accept each individual accordingly.

I have lost many friends because they did not accept me for who I have become. In fact some thought it was just a phase while others thought it was an act. Little did they know I was transitioning into the person that I was created to be.

You must learn to accept each person. If you don't feel like you can remain friends with them then don't. No one ever said that we all have to be best friends but we do need to love and respect the decision that each person makes.

Change is not always bad. In fact some changes are beneficial to your entire family. The truth of the matter is that whether you realize it or not someone is looking up to you. Someone sees something inside of you that you don't see in yourself and they are patiently waiting to see if you will be bold enough to change so that they could be courageous enough to change as well.

You may not see yourself as a role model or mentor but there is someone watching you. You have to understand that not everyone will hear the voice of God, not everyone will be able to interpret dreams or see visions. You may in fact be the only Jesus that someone sees.

When you accept others for who they have become you are showing love towards your neighbor. In fact you are implementing Christ-like behavior.

Remember someone is always watching and taking notes to how you treat others and your reaction to the changes that your neighbor makes. You must accept others just as your heavenly father has accepted you.

The power of life and death is in the tongue. Speak well of others. Encourage them to seek change and if your brother or sister needs help along the way be that light that they follow as they get closer to Christ.

Ecclesiastes 4:9-10 states: "Two are better than one, because they have a good return for their work; If one falls down, his friend can help him up. But pity the man who falls and has no one to help him up!"

CHAPTER 26

Unveil the person beneath the mask

Ten years of memorable moments and precious memories have gone by yet I feel as though I still do not know who this person truly is. We speak occasionally on the telephone and see one another frequently. No matter how much time we spend apart when we are together it always feels like the first moment we met. We both have the same interest and there seems to be a common bond amongst us. Yet I feel like this person has not yet taken off the mask so that I can see beneath it.

There is a discerning spirit that is felt anytime something doesn't seem to be quite right. I don't know if this particular person feels intimidated by me or what the real reason is, but they do indeed cover up every time we are in the presence of one another.

Little do they know, I already know that they are hiding beneath a mask and have not yet taken it off. I already know that who they portray to be is far from who they are. In fact who they are is the person that I truly adore yet with the mask they seem to be fake and I like most people I encounter, don't like phonies.

So why not unveil the person beneath? One word; fear.

We seem to be fearful of what people will think of us. Scarred that no one will like and appreciate the real person that we are. So we wake up every morning put on our mask and walk aimlessly out of the door into the world.

Right now we will all take a moment to unveil who we are. We will stop pretending that we are holier than thou, stop perpetrating to be something that we are not and we will refrain from being who we think people want us to be.

We will walk out with our naturally beautiful faces and we will be ourselves. If being yourself means you don't laugh at every joke you hear, fine. If being yourself means you have to stand against the crowd and walk a narrow path, great. If being yourself means that you lose some so called friends, even better.

When Jesus walked this earth he did not walk around with a mask, in fact he walked around freely and though he was persecuted he didn't let it hinder his walk. Jesus knew that if he had no one else on his side he had his father.

Someone right now is waiting patiently for a chance to get to know the real you. Unveil the person you are. You can't run with a mask on. There comes a time when you have to lay aside every weight so that you can freely run your race in life.

To this day I still patiently wait for the person I encountered ten years ago to take off their mask. For unknown reasons they still feel as though they have to cover up who they are. I will wait until they are ready to show themselves freely because I know that beneath their mask and beneath your mask is a unique person dying to come out and show who you truly are.

CHAPTER 27

Be Free

I always did say that there is no way that I would have made it through slavery. Those poor helpless people were sold to the highest bidder then forced to live their lives under the leadership of someone who in fact was no better than they were. Slaves had to get up and work the fields and take orders from sunrise to sunset without complaining. They were separated from loved ones and beaten at the wake of dawn. It was as though they had no voice and unfortunately no freedom.

Slavery has been over, thank God, for many years. Yet some of us still walk in the slave mentality. We forget that man does not own us and that we don't have to walk in fear of getting sold to the highest bidder.

We are free. We can work at any corporation and run for any office. There are not any limits to how high we can fly. Jesus has already paid the ultimate price for us.

You will never be truly free until your mind has been set free. Your mind is an essential part of your being and you need your mind to be regulated by God daily, in fact for some of us we need a regulated mind every hour on the hour. Thankfully God is the only one with the power to keep our minds from going astray. We must be strong enough to know that we have the power to cast down any illusions, doubt, and fear. In fact we must be willing to let God replace our fear with his faith, doubt with deliverance, pain with peace, worry with worship, hurt with healing, fornication with forgiveness, jealousy with joy, lust with true love, and sin with the savior.

It takes a lot of time spent with God to understand just how powerful he is and how he is truly able to break any strongholds in our life.

I don't know personally what it is that is keeping you from being free but I do know that there is nothing to hard for God. But you have to believe for yourself. You have to study the bible and be willing to follow the narrow path that is placed before you.

Let me ask you a question. If the police knocked on your door and informed you that there was a vacancy at the federal prison and they are in need of volunteers to spend the next twenty years incarcerated with someone watching your every move from the time you wake up to the time you go to bed, monitoring your telephone calls and they will only give you scheduled visits with family and friends, would you agree to those terms and become a ward of the state? I would imagine that you would immediately decline the offer. You would choose to be free.

Being free means you are not restricted and you have the power to choose your actions. In other words you are not in bondage, slavery has come and gone, you are free to make conscious decisions on your own behalf.

Free your mind of evil thoughts and live each day as though it is the first day of the best day of the rest of your life.

Philippians 3:12 states: "Not that I have already obtained all this, or have already been made perfect, but I press on to take hold of that for which Christ Jesus took hold of me."

I dare you to let loose of whatever stronghold has your mind and take hold to Jesus. He is more than able to give you what you need to run your race in this life.

Be unique. Be bold. Be courageous. Be gentle. Be patient. Be a trailblazer. Be joyful. Be loving. Be kind. Be self-confident. Be fearless. Be yourself. Be free.

CHAPTER 28

Walk in Spirit and in Truth

While attending an out of the city church I heard this preacher preach for the first time. Now I must admit that I am very selective about whom I listen to preach. It's one thing when I am at my home church and there are different respected ministers and visiting ministers that minister the word but when I actually leave the city I usually only go and listen to those that I have already heard previously, as I don't want to drive a distance for someone other than my own pastor or home church ministers. In fact there was a time that I would only listen to my pastor preaching the word. Anytime that he was not preaching the word at church I would leave immediately after giving my tithes and offering. I know that wasn't right as God can use anyone to preach his word but I genuinely love hearing my pastor. And I must admit that even though I would love to hear Pastor Lloyd Joiner Jr., preach every Sunday, I have now grown enough in the word to willingly listen to others proclaim the word of God.

Nonetheless I attended this out of the city church with the anticipation that I would hear the preacher that was advertised in the announcements but to my surprise I learned once I made it to the respected church that I had somehow gotten my dates mixed up. I decided to stay and receive whomever God led to give the word that night. I must admit that I was thoroughly impressed with the minister of the hour as the sermon was exactly what I needed to hear and it felt as if it was directed towards me.

I left that night feeling renewed and ready to take on the world. The minister that night really spoke in the spirit and had an amazing anointing placed on his life. To my surprise approximately two weeks later I met the minister that spoke that night again. He introduced himself accordingly and invited me to a local conference where he was speaking. Again he amazed me as his sermon was simply beautiful and spirit filled.

We became friends and began getting to know one another. To my surprise though he walked amazingly in the spirit he did not walk well in truth. In fact once I began getting to know him personally my stomach turned by the fact that he did not take the time to practice what he preached. Now don't get me wrong I am no fool and I totally understand that we must discern the minister from the man which simply means that the person you see in the spirit is not of himself but is under the anointing of God yet when you see him outside of the church he is of himself, but hopefully still following God and still filled with God's power.

The only problem with this man was that he walked in spirit but not in truth. We must learn to walk in spirit and in truth. You can't be one way inside the house of the Lord and a totally different way outside. Don't straddle the fence. God has thought enough of you to send his only son to die on your behalf so that you may live a life that is pleasing and acceptable.

Life is not always easy in fact it is sometimes hard as hell. But everyday that you choose to follow God wholeheartedly is a day of peace and happiness. Because God can give you what man never will be able to. God is able to give you inner peace for your soul and convict you in your wrong doing. He is able to walk with you in spirit and in truth and guide you along your way. You have to make a conscious decision today and follow his voice and answer his call. Choose this day whom you will serve. And when you choose God, as I know you will, follow him full heartedly with all of your heart, mind, body, and soul.

I chose to walk in spirit and truth and I must admit that it is by far the best decision that I have ever made.

CHAPTER 29

Take the Chains off your hands and Shackles off of your Feet

There is a church where the spirit of the Lord is in that place; there are great sounds of dancing and shouting. That church is filled with praises and songs of Zion. The atmosphere is already set and deliverance is in order. The only problem is that ninety nine point nine percent of the congregation is held down by chains on their hands and shackles on their feet.

You wait patiently for Sunday morning service yet when you are in the right place at the right time you are too afraid to let loose and let the spirit of God overtake you. Some are afraid of who may be looking and what others will say.

May I remind you that when you go to the house of the Lord you are going there for one reason and one reason alone; God. You do not go to check out who is wearing the latest fashion or which woman will set beside which man. Nor do you go to hear your favorite choir member sing your favorite church song. And if you are concerned about who is looking at you and what they may say if they see you praise the Lord than you are concerned with the wrong thing because truth be told if someone else has the time to watch what you are doing during service in church it may be because they are not praising God themselves. When you truly give praise you don't have time for foolishness because your mind is steadfast on God and getting closer to his presence.

The word of God says that the closer you draw to God, the closer God will draw to you. You can't draw closer to go with chains on your hands and shackles on your feet. You have to take them off and freely give yourself to your father. You may be in the right place to get your deliverance but you have to let go and let God minister to you whether through song, preaching, or his still quiet voice.

James 4:7states, "Submit yourselves, then, to God. Resist the devil, and he will flee from you." You must submit to God at all times because unfortunately the devil shows up in the church. He will come in any way, shape, or form and do whatever he has to in order to get your focus off God. When you resist the enemy and his evil tactics it is then that you are able to focus on God and not man.

Without the chains you are able to lift up holy hands and freely give yourself away. Without shackles you are able to release your entire body to the Lord. You have to be a willing participate. All too often we want God to do his part as well as ours. I know you have faith but it is time that you activate your faith in God.

I love being in the house of the Lord as often as possible but there is a certain season that I truly wait patiently for and that is, the season of revival. There is an anticipation of revival that people receive in which they show up with expectancy. Revival is that time of renewing, refreshing, and reviving and it often seems that the spirit of the Lord is walking down every aisle and touching on every pew. During revival it seems as though all of our burdens are laid down at the altar and everyone anticipates a move from God.

Revival is an amazing time for Christians but can I tell you that God is the same at all times. The same God that blessed you at last year's revival is the same God that is more than able to bless you during Sunday morning worship, Monday evening at work, Tuesday while riding in your car, Wednesday night praise, Thursday morning while eating breakfast, Friday night prayer meeting, and Saturday evening shopping. He is a God that is on call all day every day waiting for you to take the chains off your hands and shackles off your feet.

CHAPTER 30

Fearlessly and Wonderfully Made

My mask is off. I don't want to run nor do I feel like hiding. I am fearfully and wonderfully made. From the crowns of my head to the soles of my feet I am better that anything you can eat that is sweet. I have overcome my past and I am proudly walking into the future. I am a force to be reckon with, a voice to be heard. I am that person that when I wake up the enemy starts trembling and demons begin to cry. I am smart, articulate, funny, and kind. I have a smile that will make every man turn my way and every woman stop and stare. I have joy in my heart, peace like a river, and more love to give than a bride on her wedding night. I am a confident, strong, loyal Christian and I refuse to fall, shake, or bend, nor will I compromise, I am a true believer saints hear my roar.

When Jesus hung on the cross he had me in mind. He never murmured a word instead he hung his head low and gracefully took his last breathe for he knew it was pre-destined for you and I to be here today. Jesus died for all people young and old, rich and poor, black and white, sinner and saint. He died because he knew that each of us had work to do. He died because he believed in the power of the father. He died for us to have a better tomorrow.

You are so beautiful I hope you can see that there is no need for a mask as it is time that you be the woman or man that God purposely created you to be. All it takes is for you to simply believe in yourself and believe in the power of your father looking down from heaven above. Don't let the death of Jesus be in vein. He was bruised for your transgressions and wounded for you and I. Jesus lived a life of perfection and chose to willingly and humbly go through temptation and beatings, harsh words and betrayal all for you to be able to have breathe in your body.

There are no more excuses, no chain or shackle holding you back. The make up is off you are truly uncovered. You have taken off the mask and now you are free. There is no need to wait for tomorrow for tomorrow is not promised. All you have is this moment. Jesus said that if we have faith as small as a mustard seed we will be able to move mountains. Well my friend, you have endured long enough. It is now time to exercise your faith and move all of the mountains in your life. Tell weeping he has to go, and doubt has to disappear. Tell jealousy you now have joy and the pain you once had is replaced with peace. Tell hate you found happiness and fear has been replaced with faith, tell bitterness to pack its' bag for you now have found something so much better. Inform gossip that you now have glory and anger that you found a God that is awesome. You no longer have betrayal in your heart because your trials have made you better and all of your tests have been turned into miraculous testimonies. So go out and tell all of the purposeful sin that you now have a marvelous Savior.

There is nothing holding you back and nothing keeping you down for you are the master of your own mind and captain of the sea. You have limitless opportunities that go as high as the beautiful sky. You can own your own business, write your own book, get a degree, become a record producer, or mayor of your city, you can pass that state test, and run for office. You are stronger than before, wiser than most, you can climb the highest mountain and swim the deepest sea. You have the victory over your enemy and can speak life over death. You now have the understanding to discern the voice of God and the faith to walk on water.

You are more than a conquer the battle has already been fought and won. You are fearfully and wonderfully made. Rejoice all of God's people for the day and time has come. Today is your day. I dare you to stand up proud and begin your journey in life after all today is the first day of the best day of the rest of your very blessed life.

FINAL BLESSING

I hope and pray that this book has helped you get closer to God. He is truly a wonder in my soul. God led me to write this book and in less than one month's time it was completely written. When God speaks; I listen. I pray that you will do the same and by faith I believe that he will give you all of the desires of your heart.

I pray that you will submit yourself unto God and allow him to show you the plans that he has for your life I pray that he will indwell all of the fruits of his spirit inside of you and you will take heed to his every call. God is real and he is more than worthy to be praised. There is no secret potion or magic trick that gets you closer to God. In fact you are as close to him right now as you will be on tomorrow because God is omnipresent. He will always be right by your side waiting with loving hands stretched to you. Choose this day whom you will serve and I promise you that it will be the best decision you will ever make.

God Bless you and may he protect you in your coming and keep you in your going. I pray that he is a light to your path and you seek him in all that you do.

To God Be the Glory.